The *Art Deco*

Adult Coloring Book

ASSEMBLED BY
MADDIE MAYFAIR

ISBN-13: 978-1517451318
ISBN-10: 1517451310

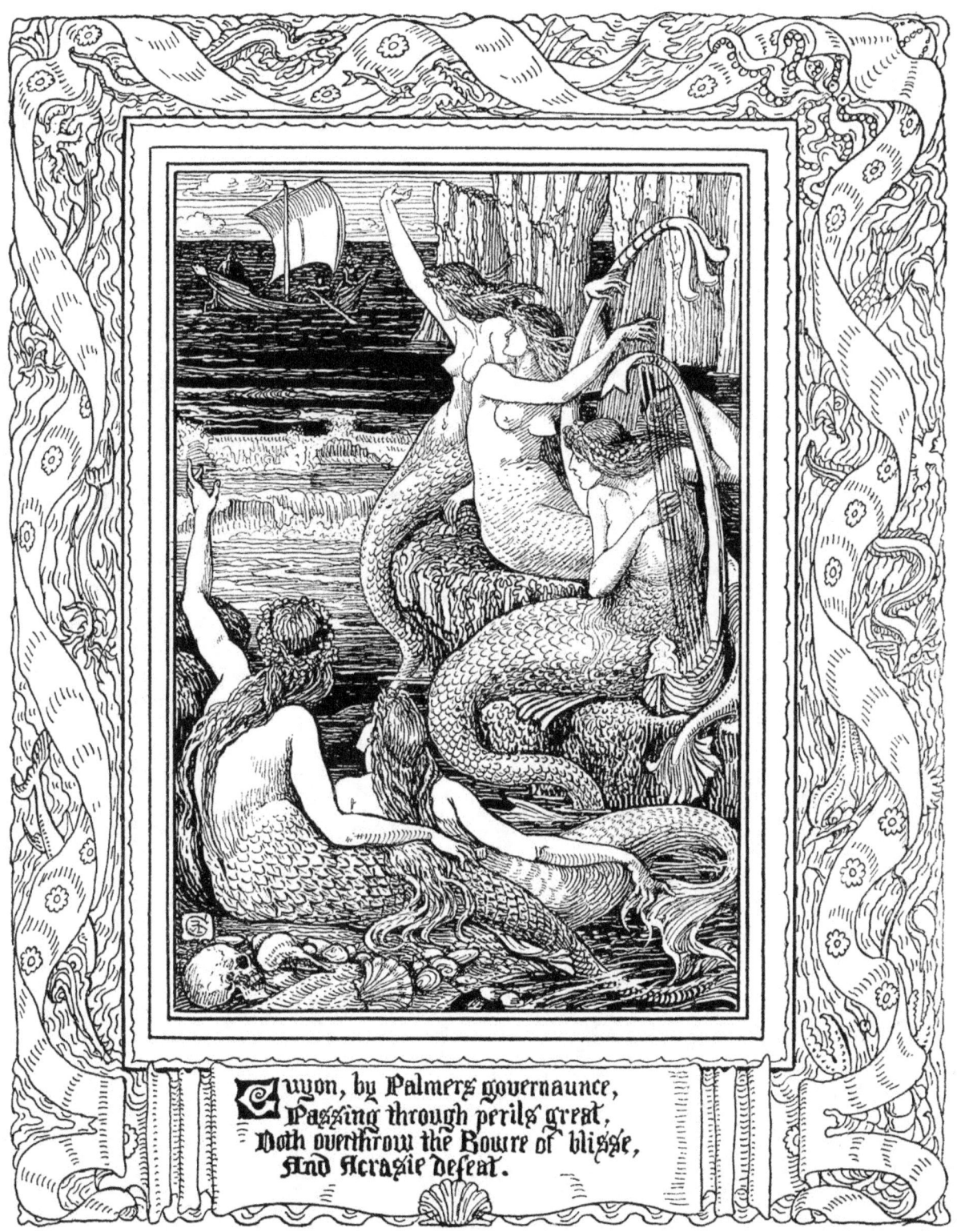

Guyon, by Palmers governaunce,
Passing through perils great,
Doth overthrow the Bowre of blisse,
And Acrasie defeat.

Bowre of Blisse. Illustration by Walter Crane (1845-1915), from the book Spenser's Faerie Queene vol. 2

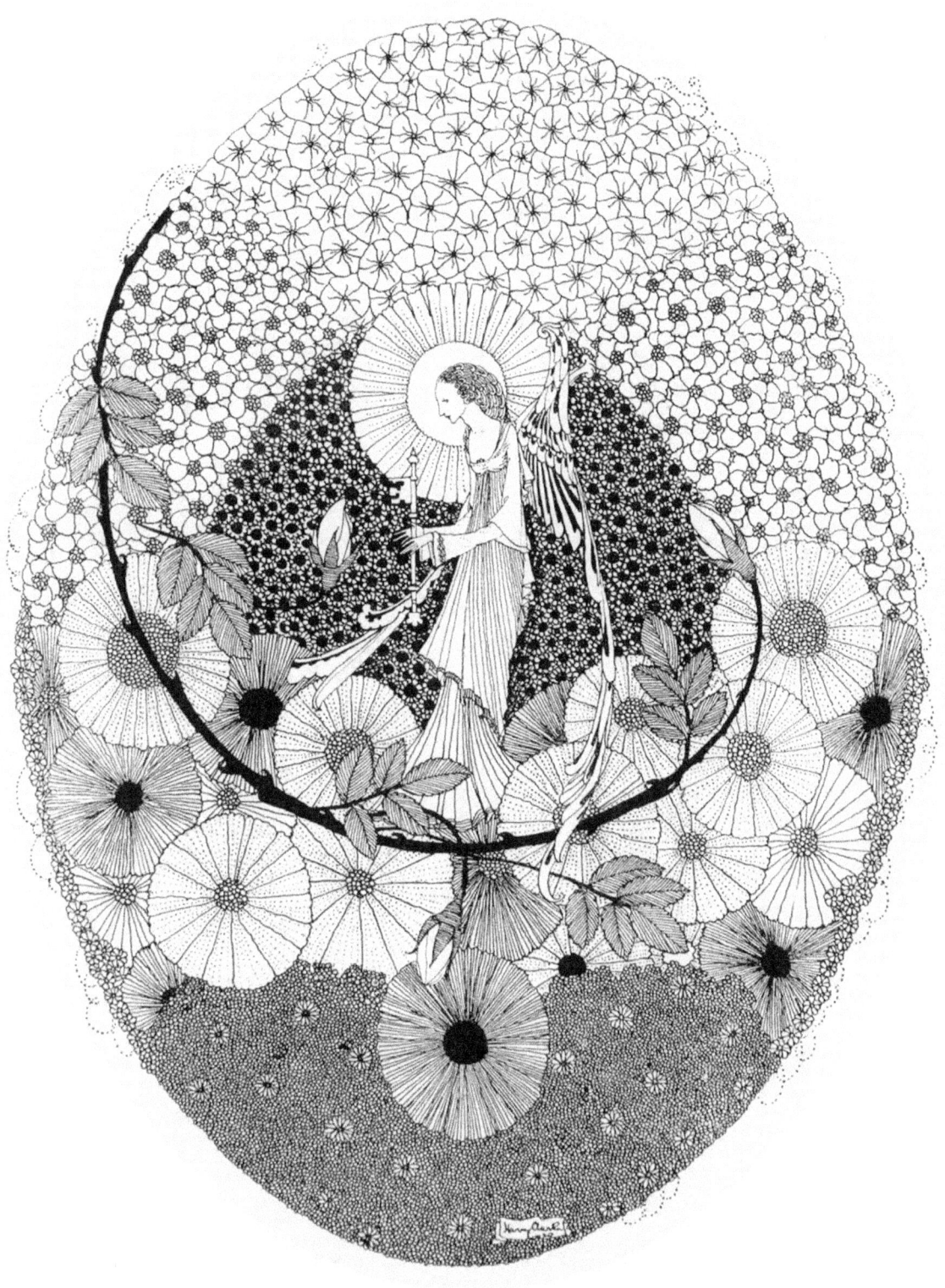

With magic key... Unlocking buds that keep the roses. Illustration by Harry Clarke (1889-1931)

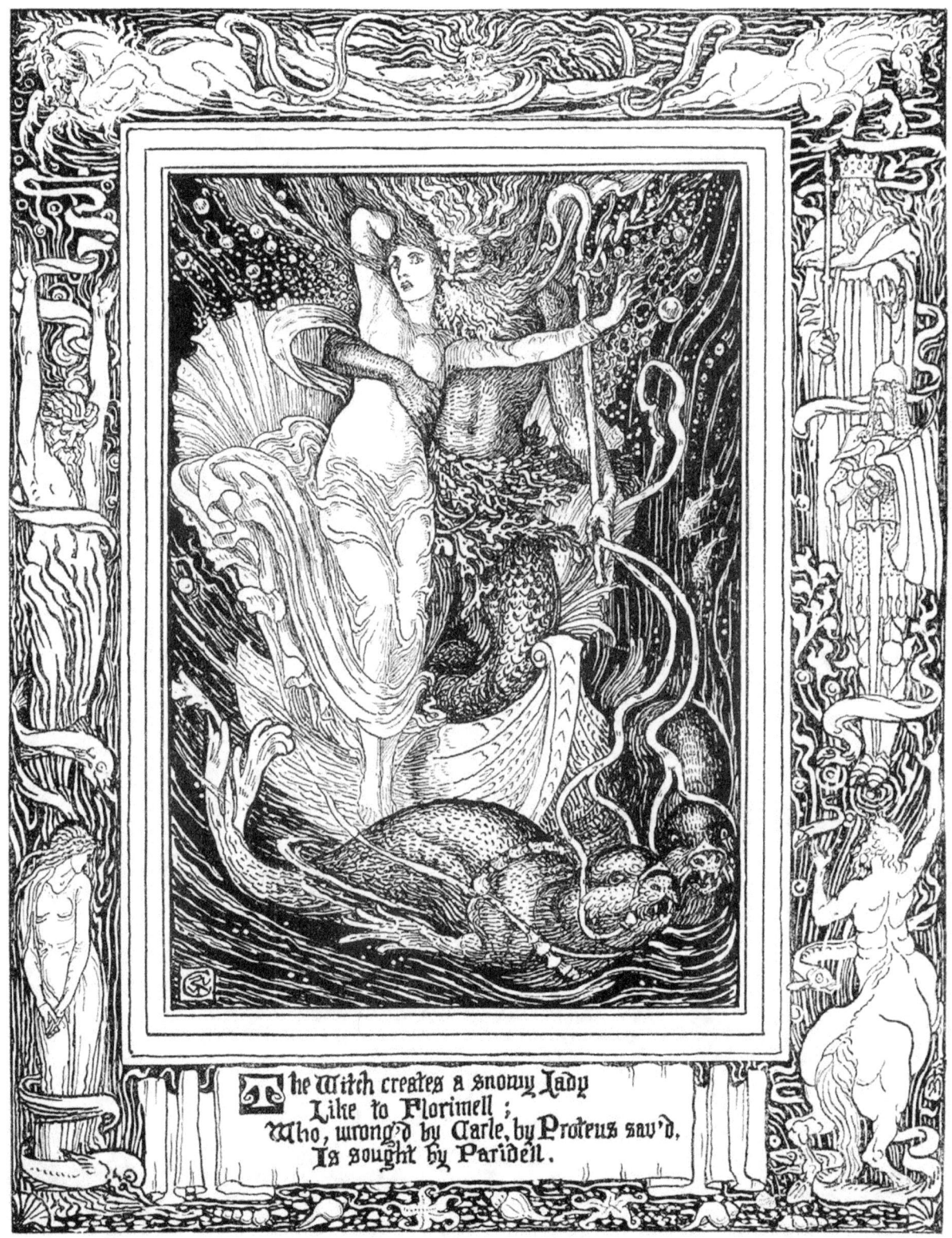

The Witch creates a snowy Lady
Like to Florimell;
Who, wrong'd by Carle, by Proteus sav'd,
Is sought by Paridell.

Snowy Lady. Illustration by Walter Crane (1845-1915), from the book Spenser's Faerie Queene vol. 2

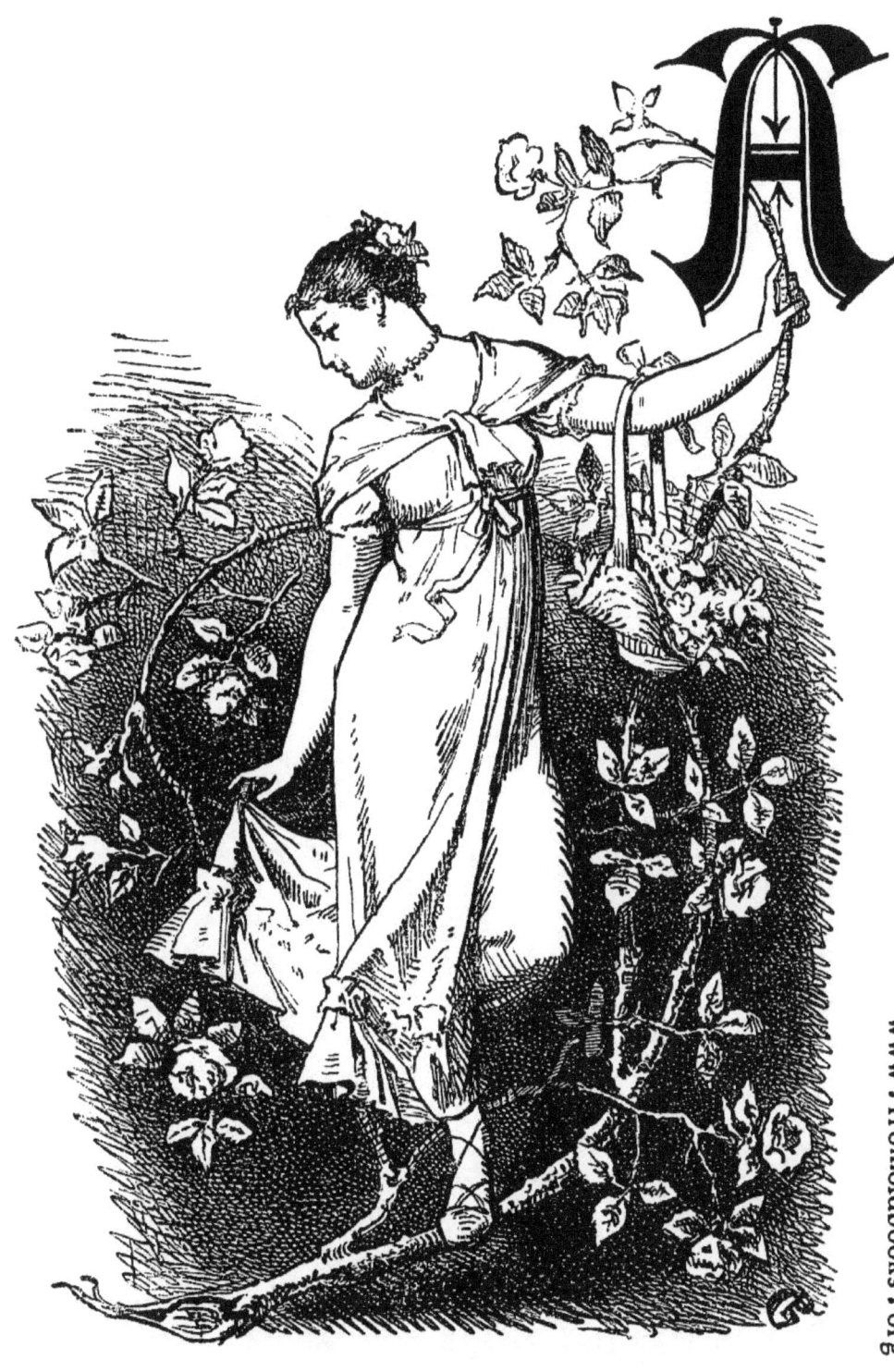

Decorative initial "A" with girl and roses. Source: Dünker, H. (Ed.): *"Goethe's Works [Goethes Werke]"* (1882)

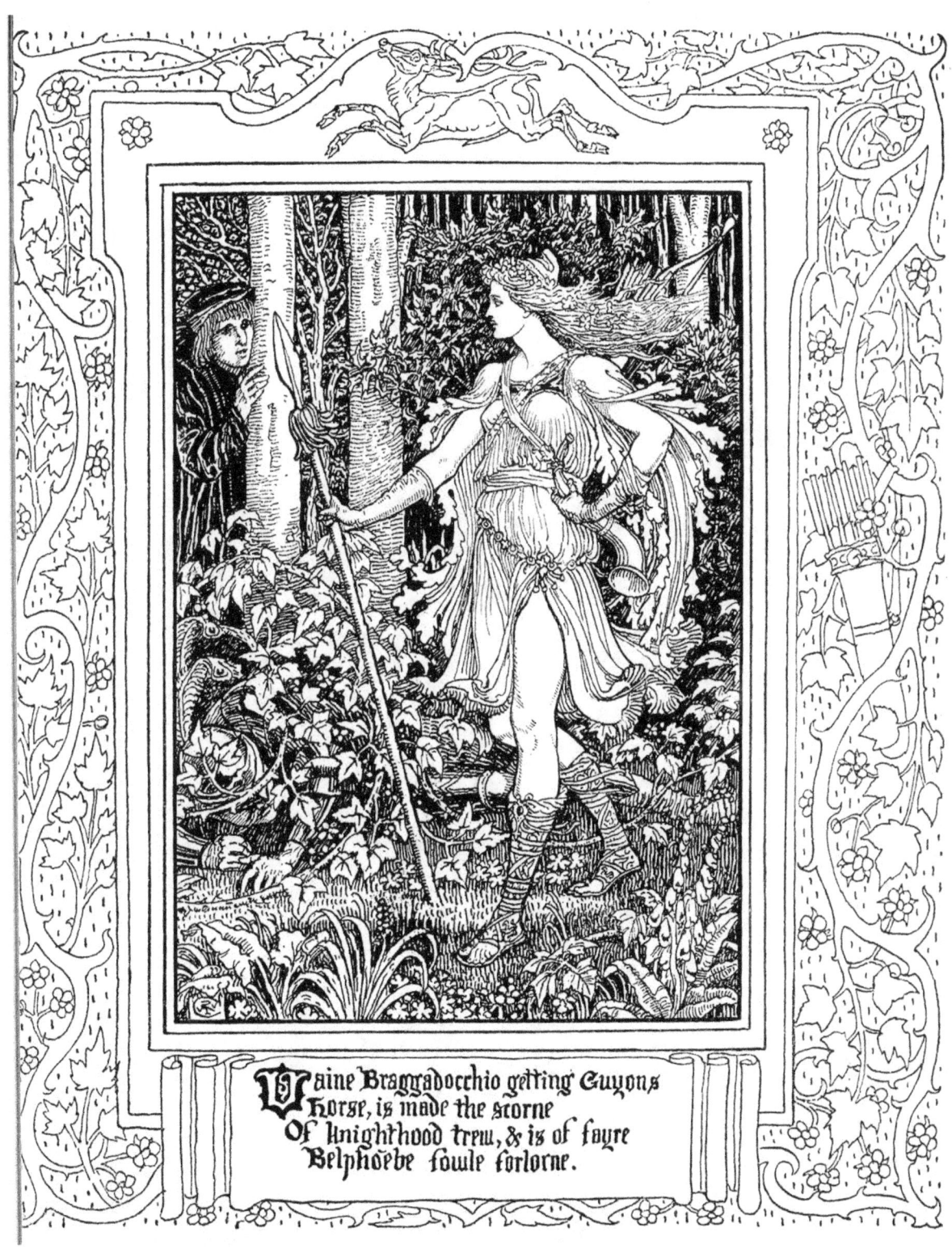

Vaine Braggadocchio. Illustration by Walter Crane (1845-1915), from Spenser's Faerie Queene, vol 2.

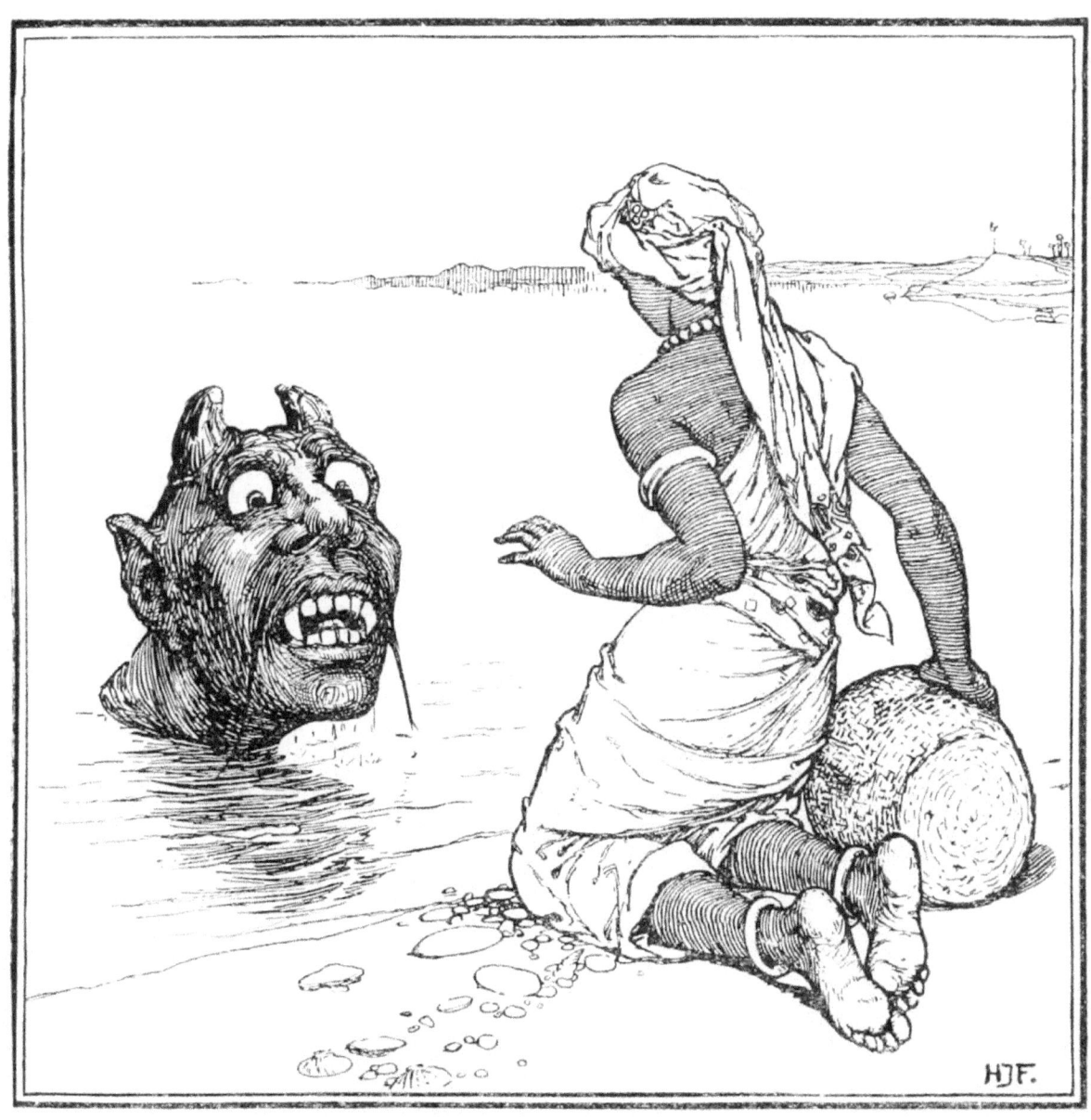

The Woman and the Ogre. Illustration by Henry Justice Ford from The Crimson Fairy Book

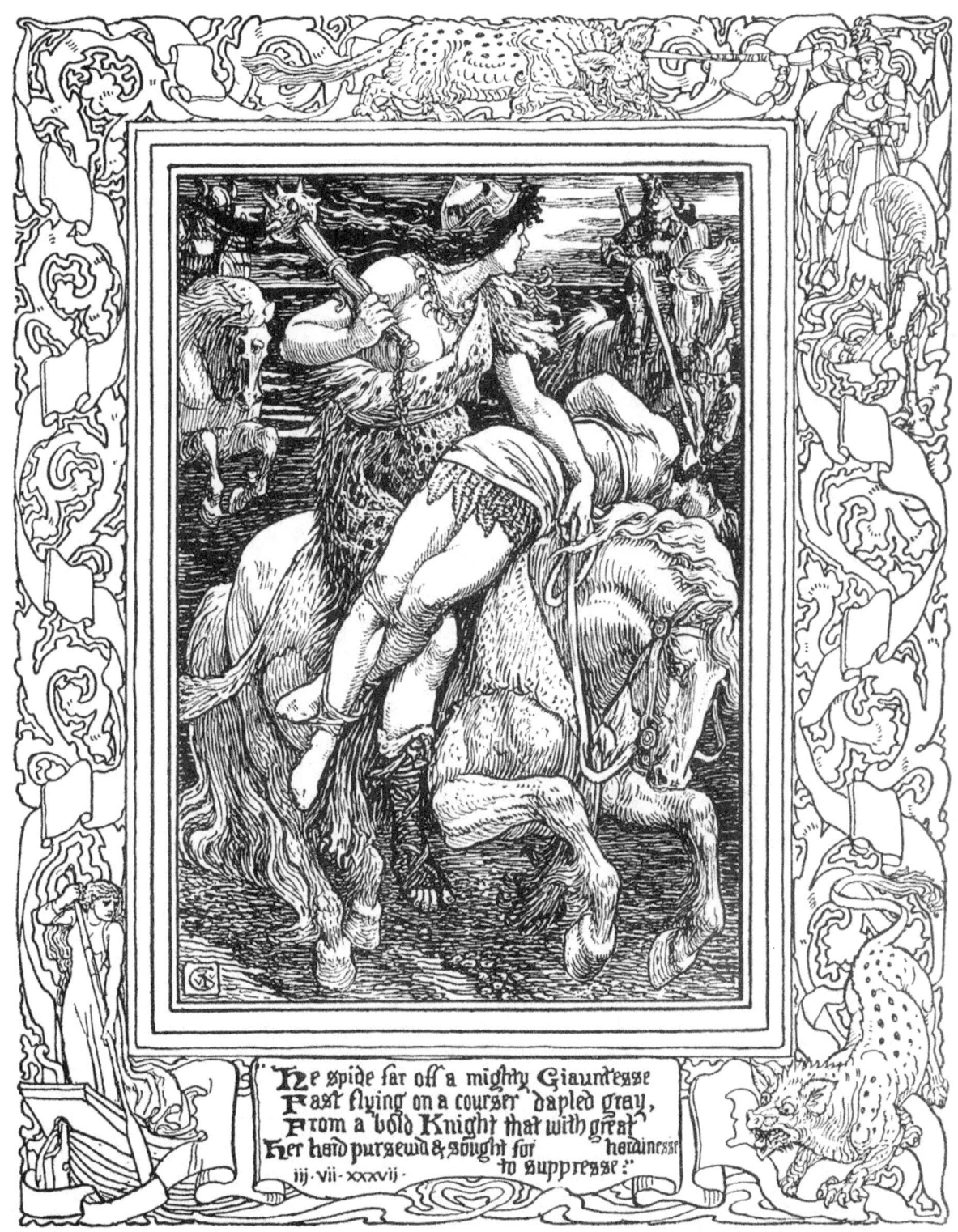

He spide far off a mighty Giauntesse
Fast flying on a courser dapled gray,
From a bold Knight that with great
Her head pursewd & sought for   hawinesse
to suppresse."
iij · vij · xxxvij ·

He Spide a Mighty Giauntesse. Illustration by Walter Crane (1845-1915), from Spenser's Faerie Queene vol. 3

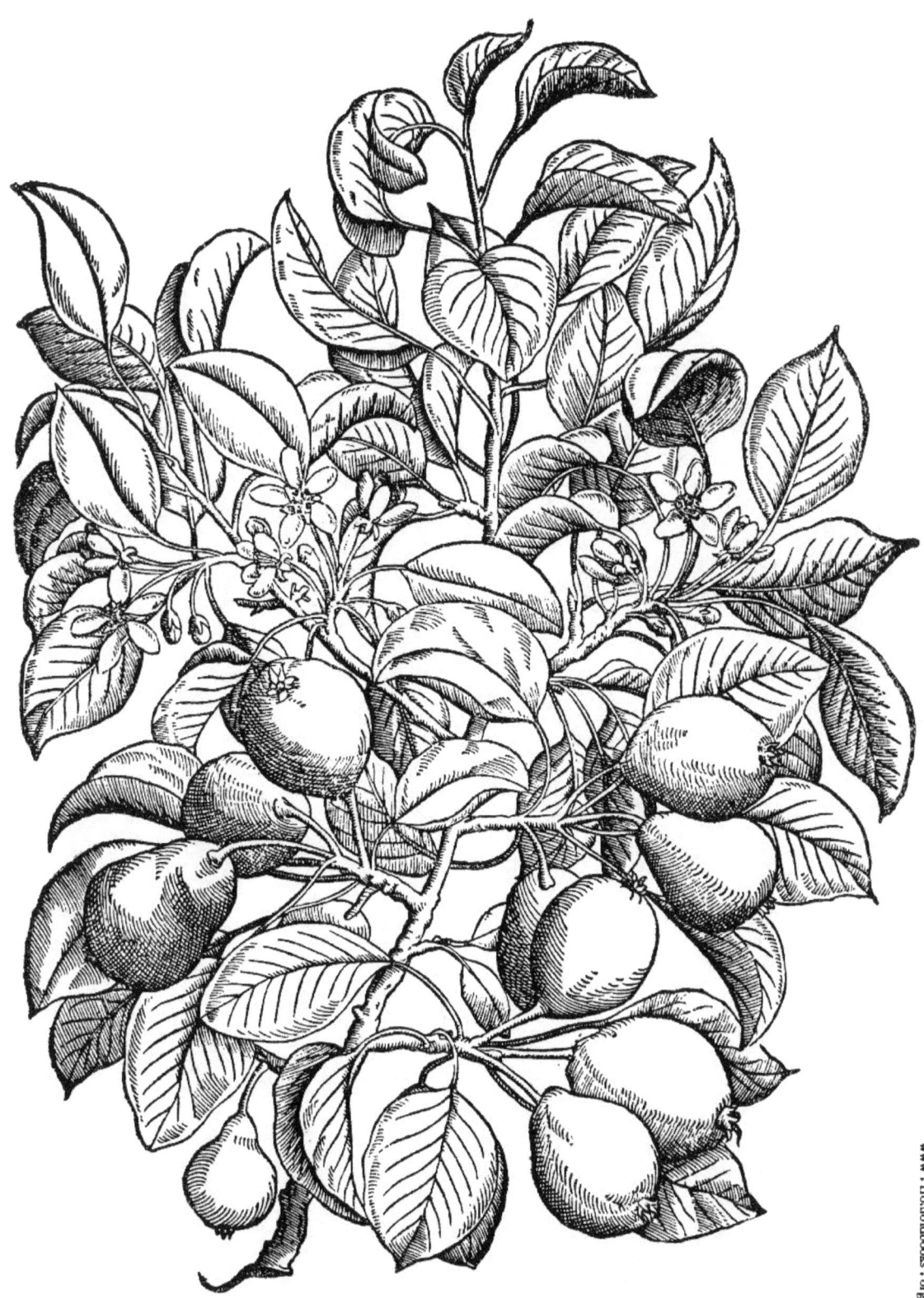

Pear. Source: Hatton, Richard G.: *"Craftsman's Plant-Book, The"* (1909)

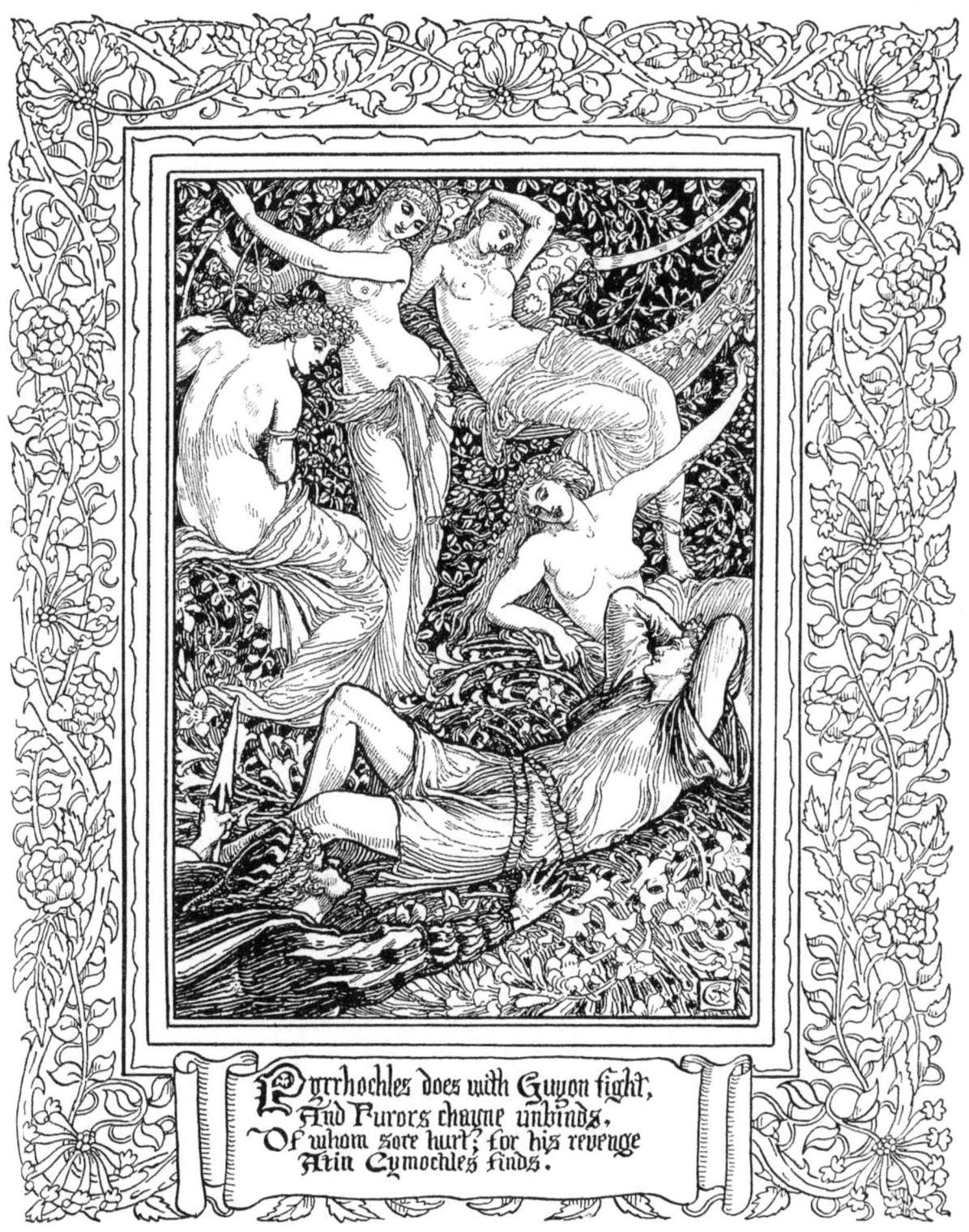

Pyrrhochles does with Guyon fight,
And Furors chayne unbinds,
Of whom sore hurt; for his revenge
Atin Cymochles finds.

Atin Cymochles Finds. Illustration by Walter Crane (1845-1915), from Spenser's Faerie Queene vol 2.

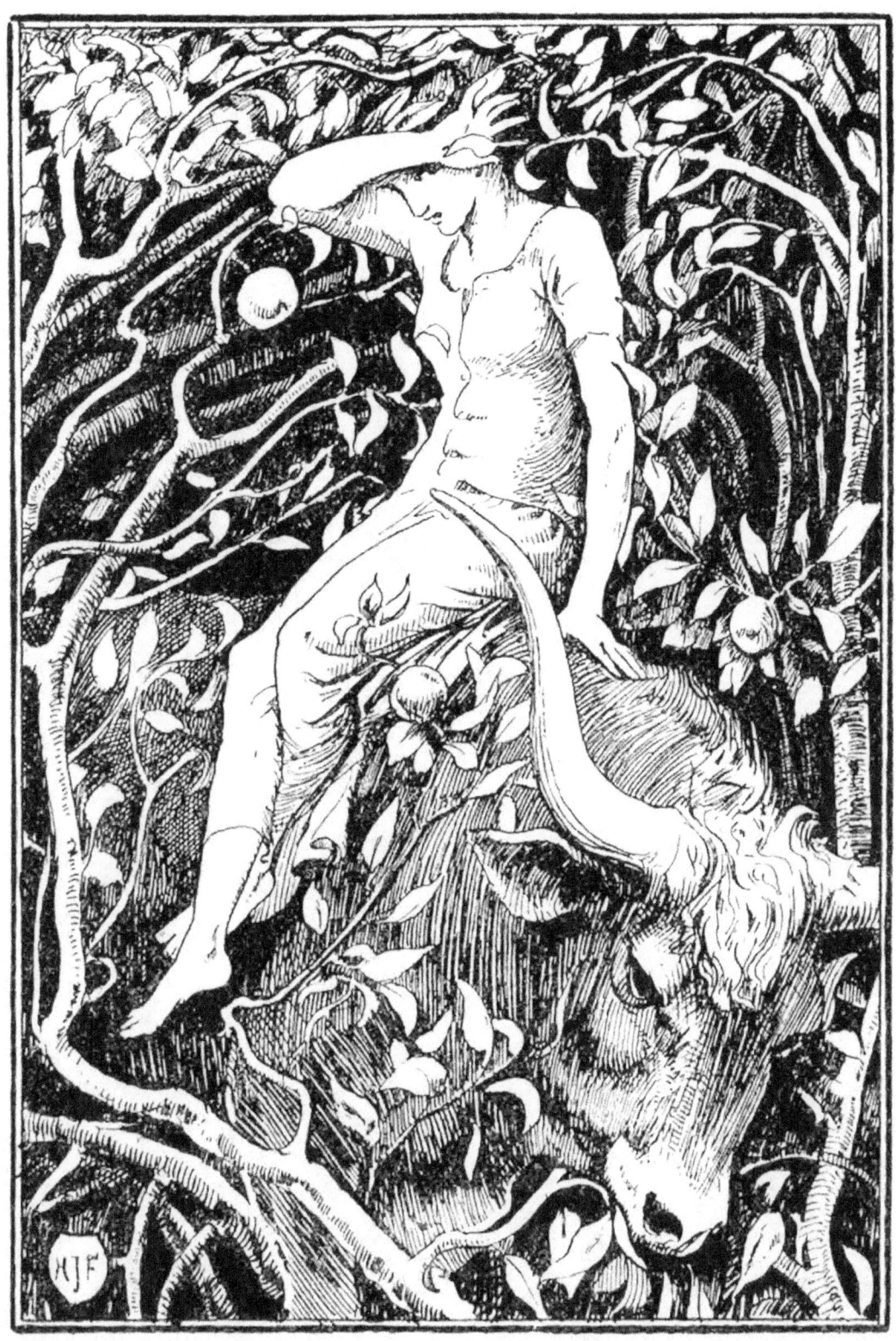

Wood Thicker and Thicker. Illustration by Henry Justice Ford (1860-1941) from The Red Fairy Book.

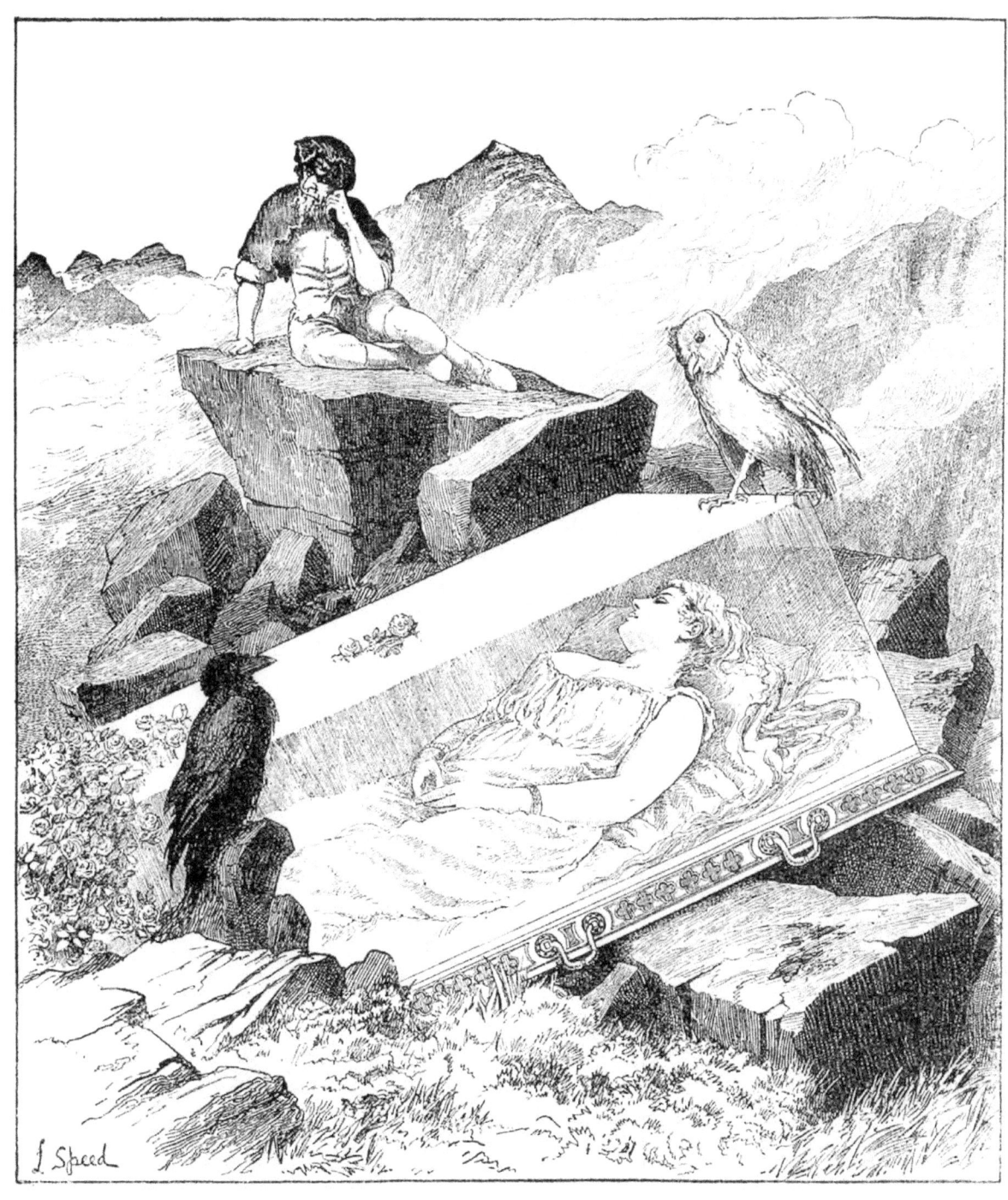

C

offin of Transparent Glass. Illustration by Lancelot Speed (1860-1931). From The Red Fairy Book.

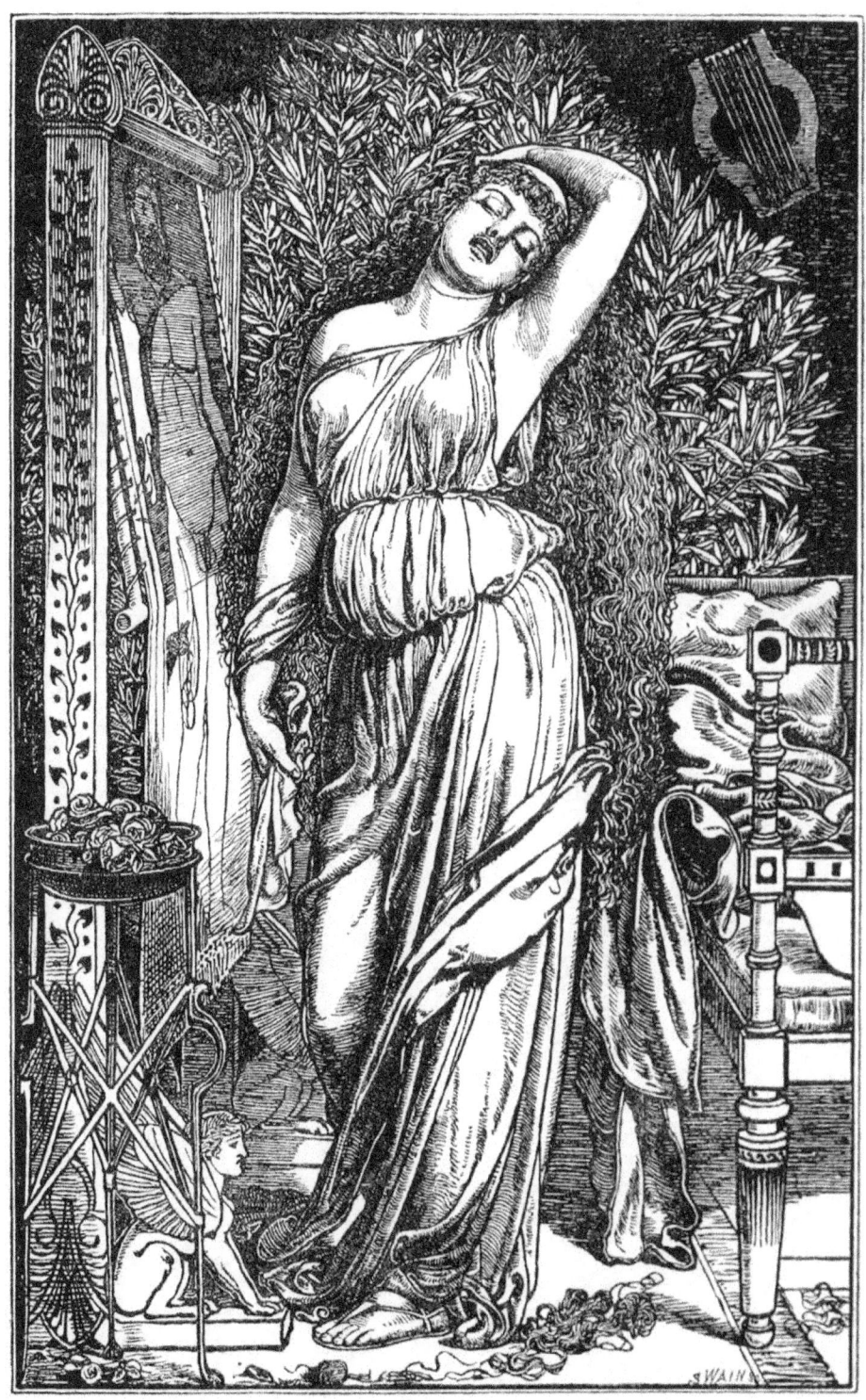

Danae in the Brazen Chamber. Illustration by Frederick Sandys (1829-1904).

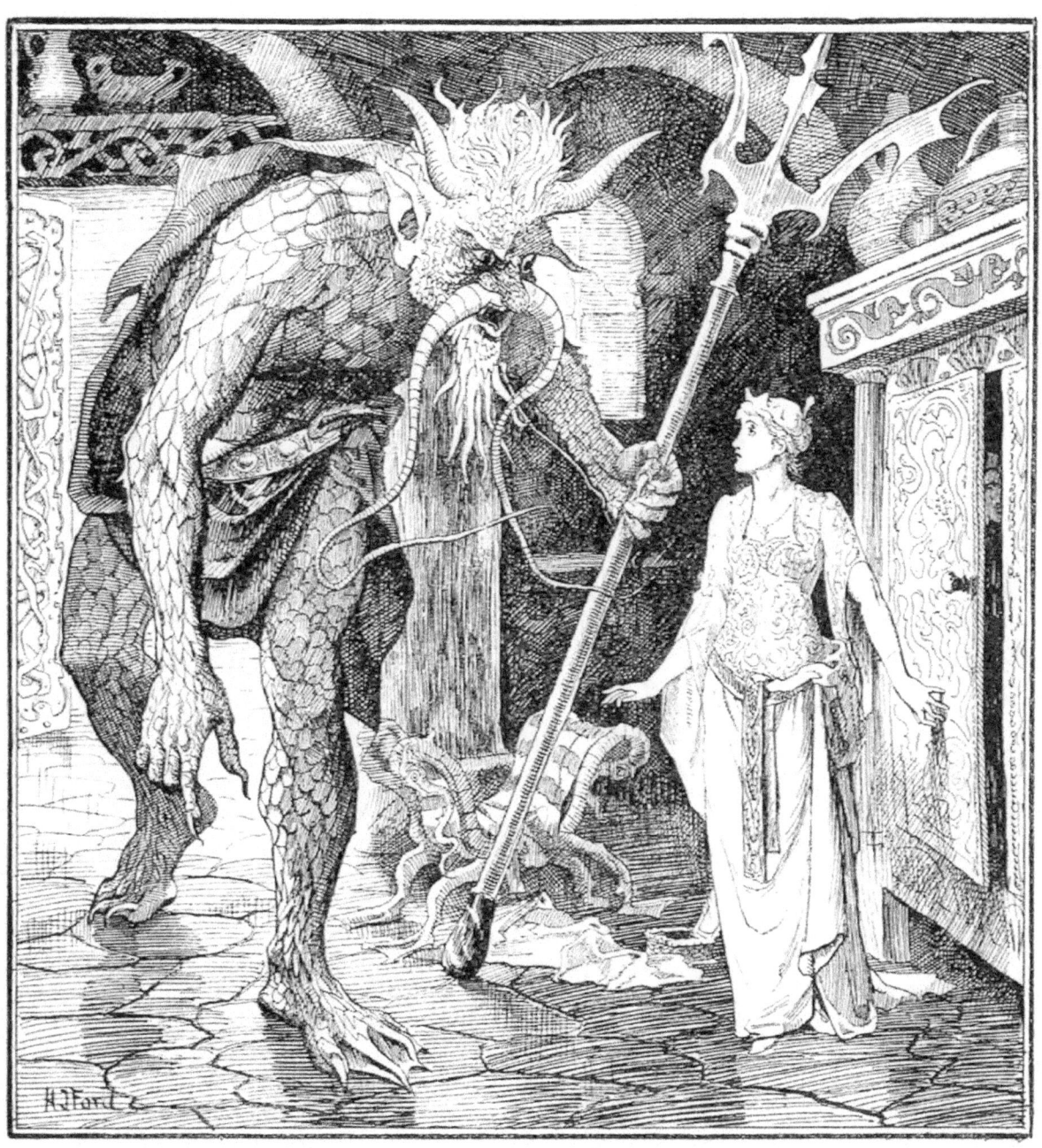

In the Cupboard. Illustration by Henry Justice Ford (1860-1941) from The Red Fairy Book.

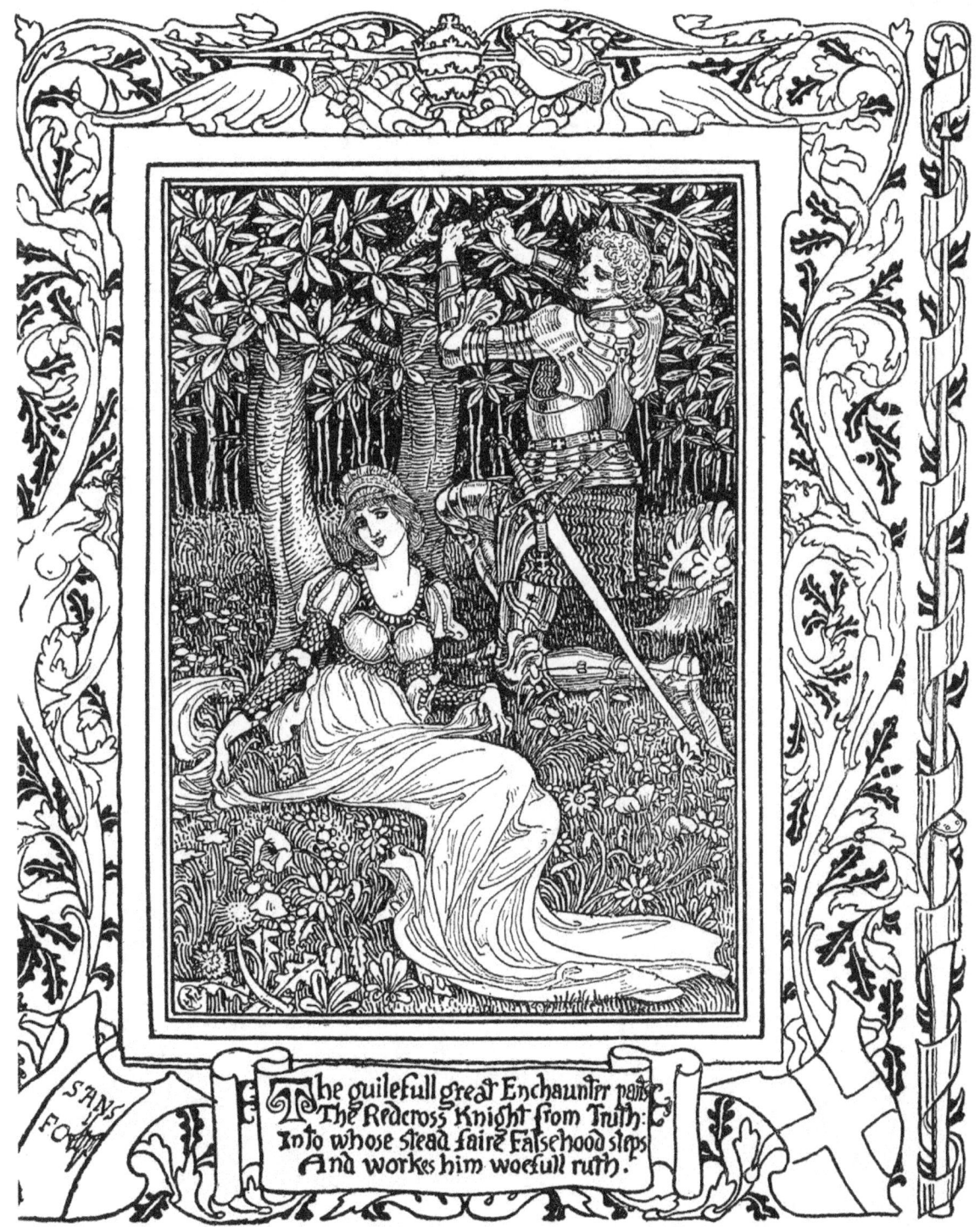

The guilefull great Enchaunter parts
The Redcross Knight from Truth:
Into whose stead faire Falsehood steps
And workes him woefull ruth.

Guileful Great Enchaunter. Illustration by Walter Crane (1845-1915), from Spenser's Faerie Queene, vol 1.

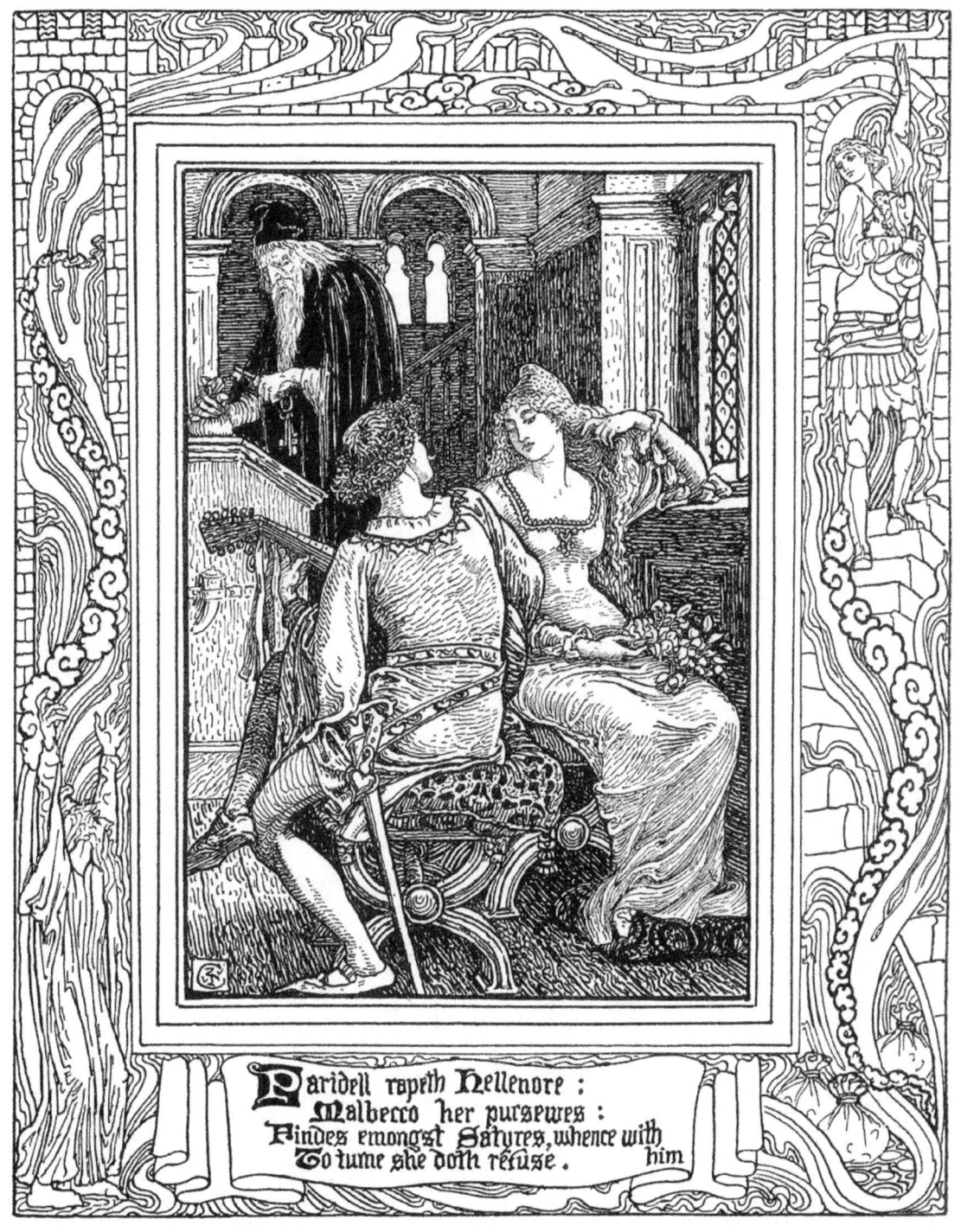

Paridell & Hellenore. Illustration by Walter Crane (1845-1915), from Spenser's Faerie Queene, vol 3.

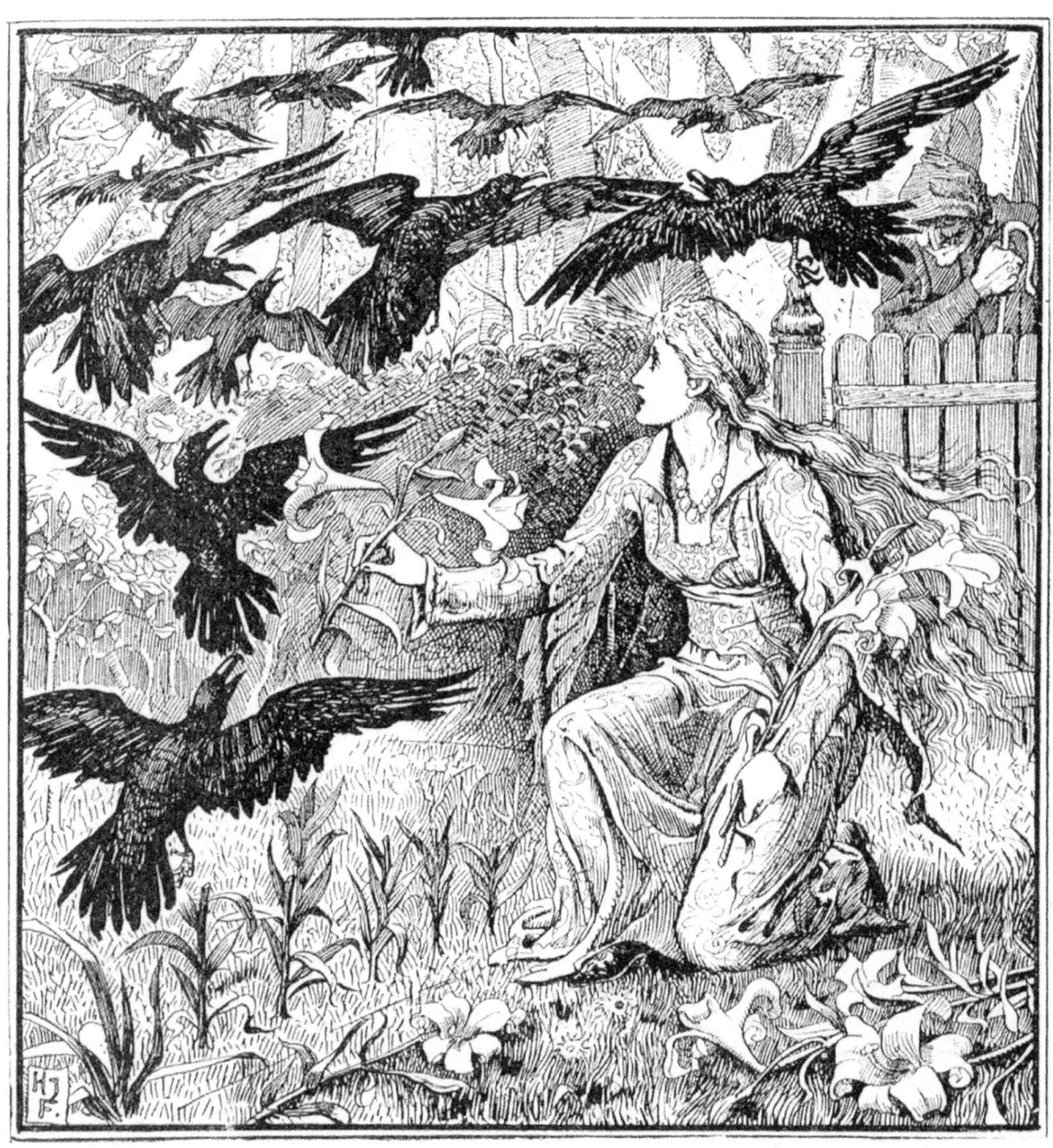

Turned into Twelve Ravens. Henry Justice Ford (1860-1941) from The Red Fairy Book

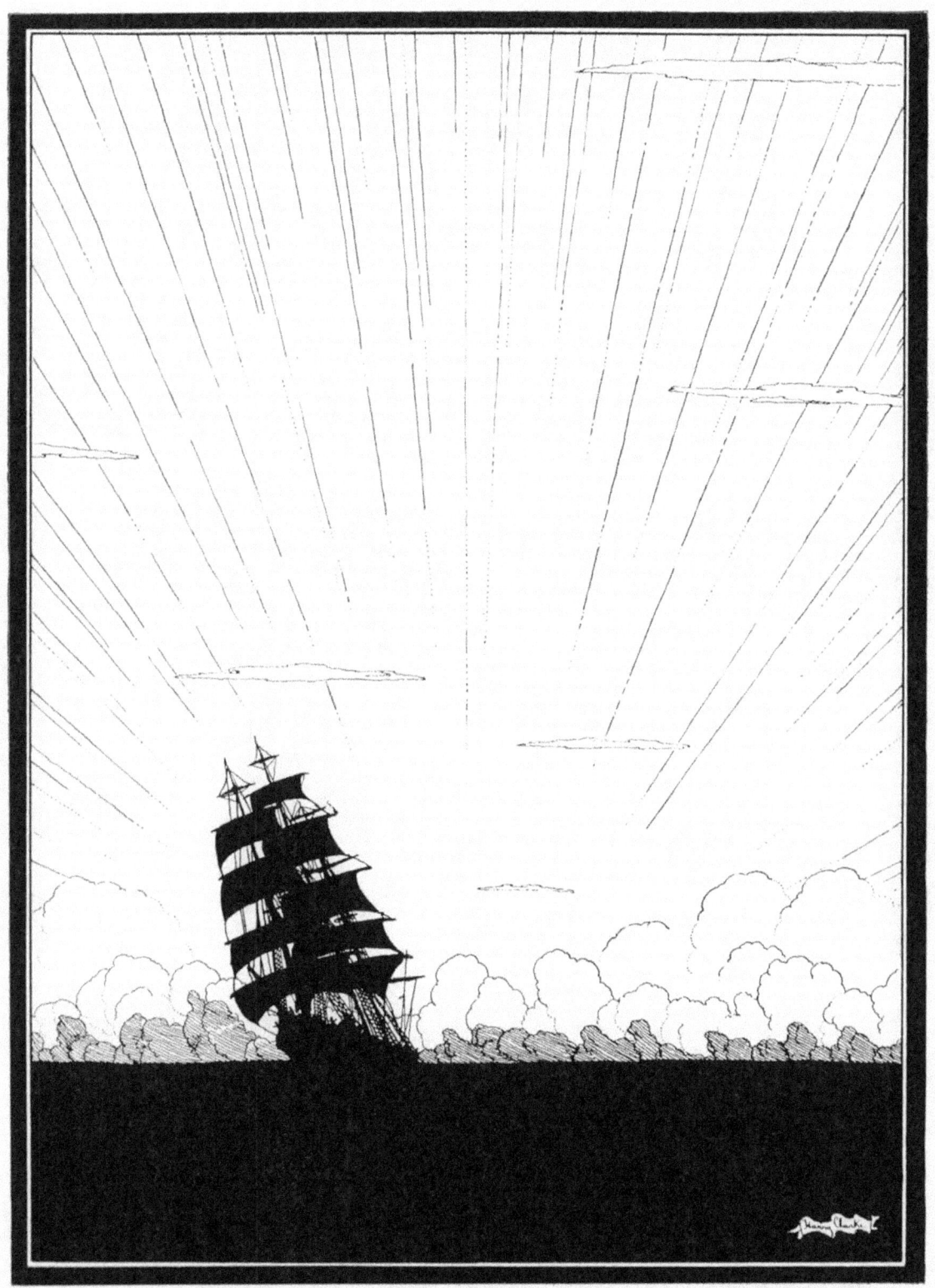

Windy Day. Illustration by Harry Clarke (1889-1931) from The Year's at the Spring.

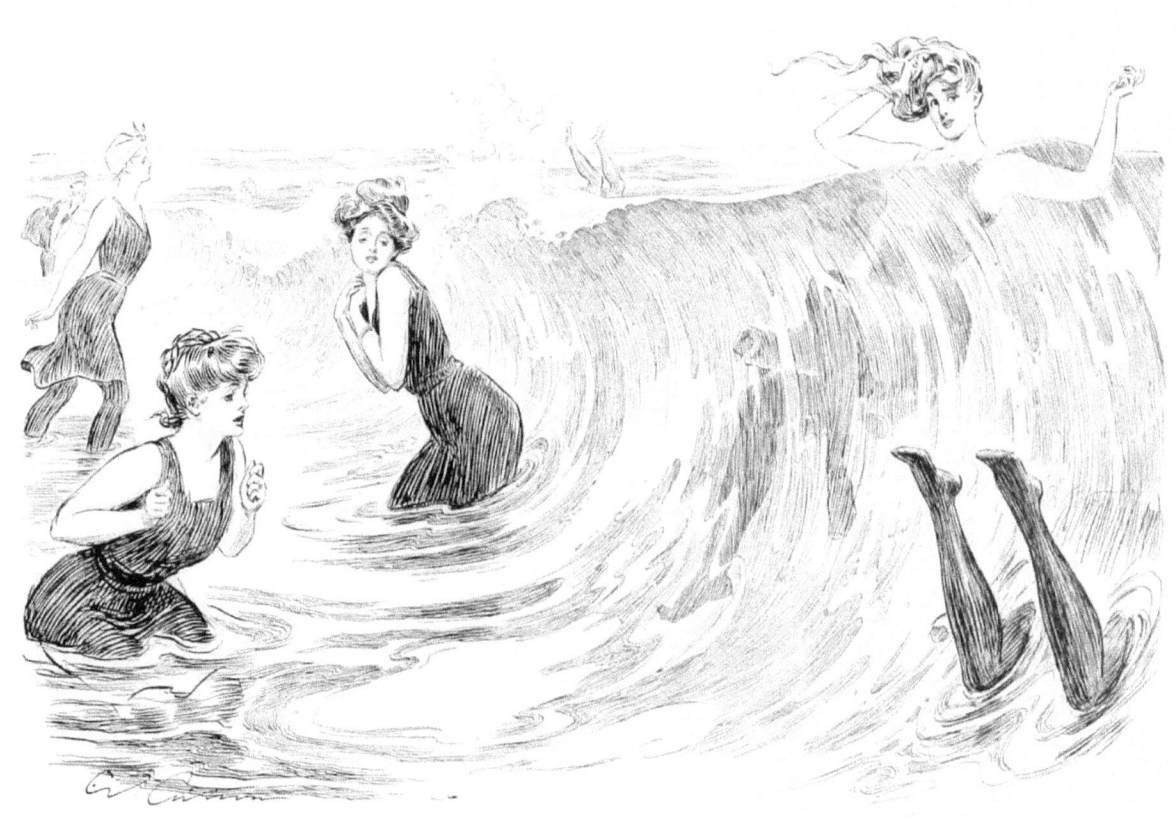

Plenty of Good Fish in the Sea. Illustration by Charles Dana Gibson (1867-1944) from The Social Ladder.

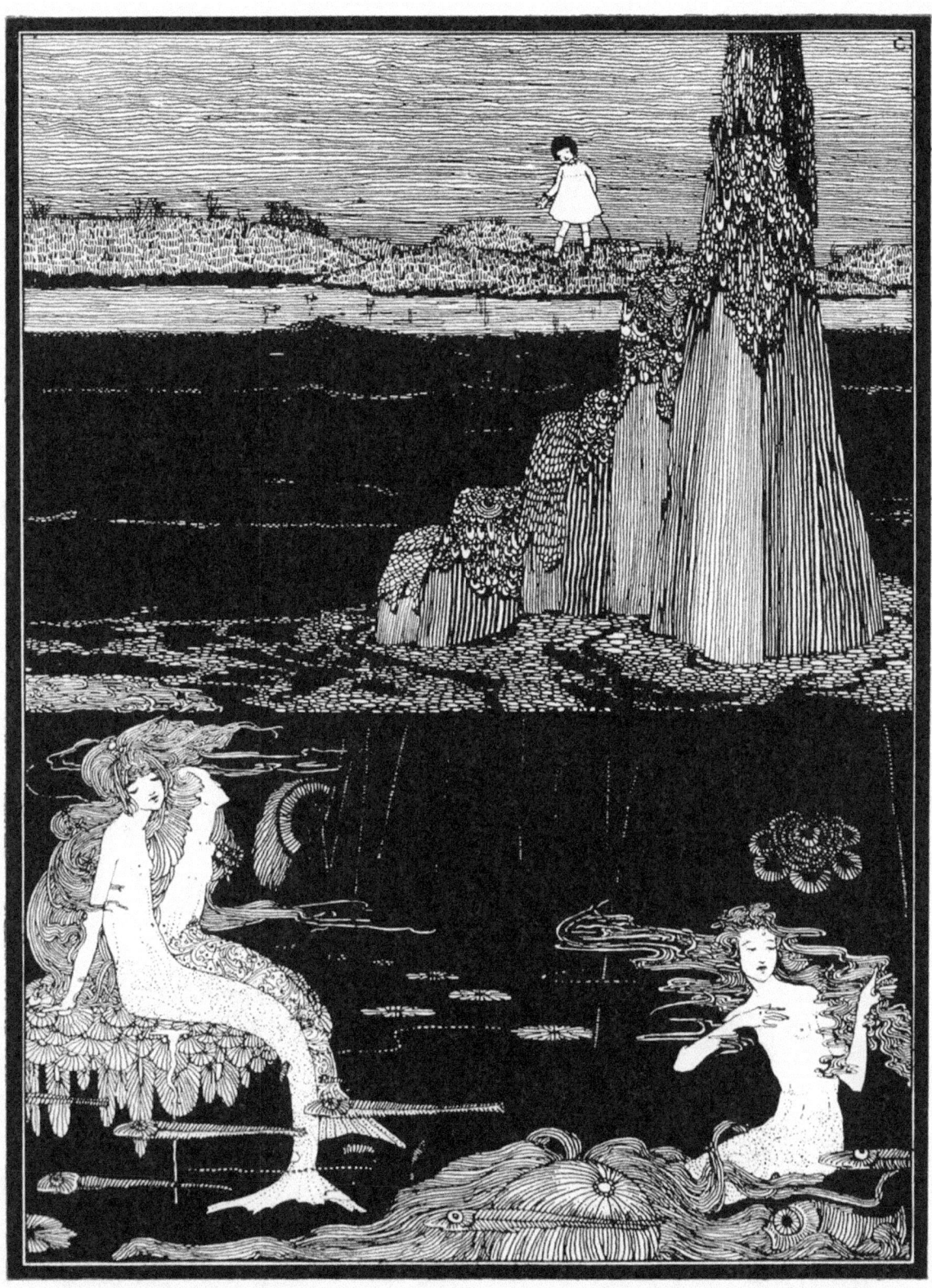

Those Rocks Amid. Illustration by Harry Clarke (1889-1931) from The Year's at the Spring.

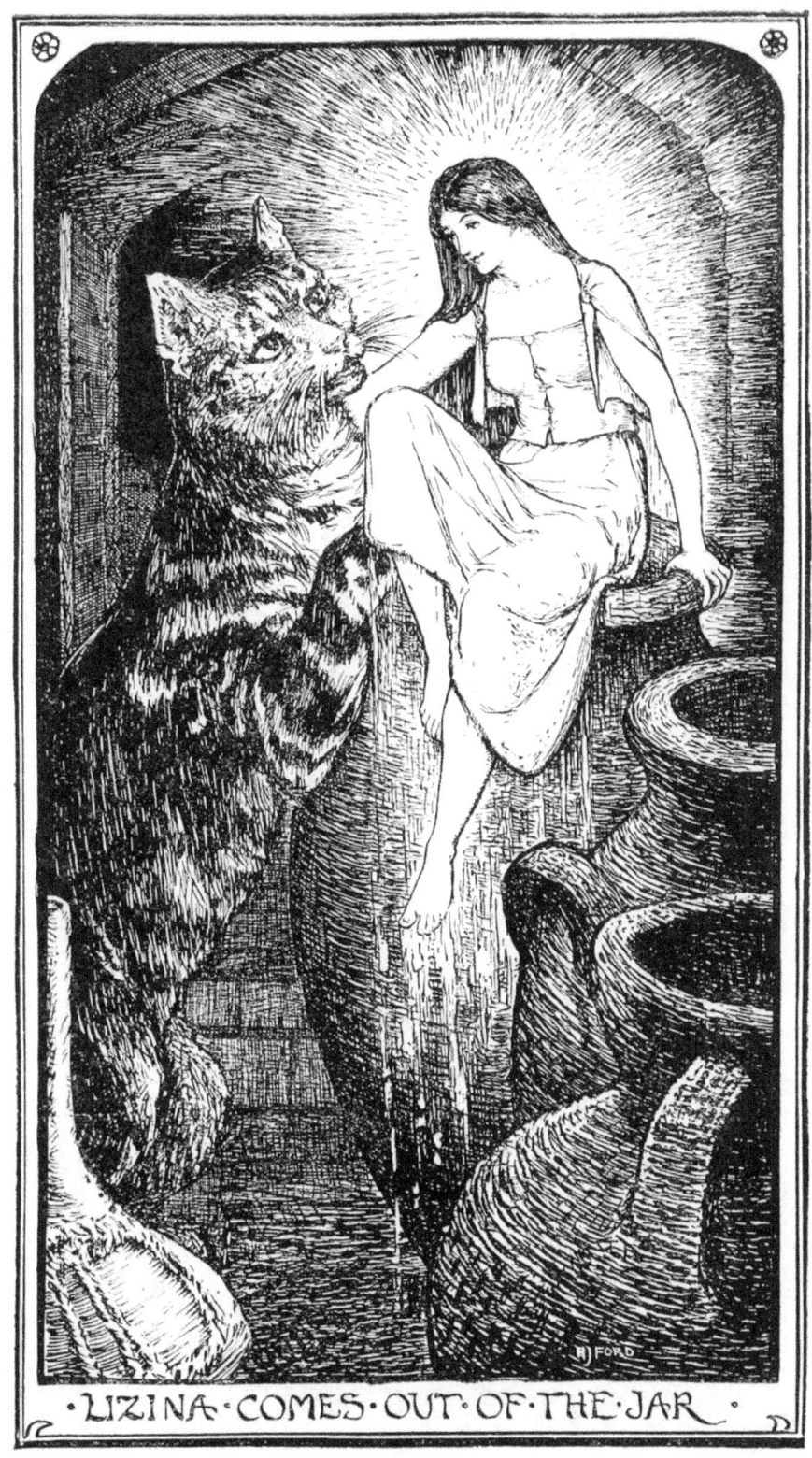

·LIZINA·COMES·OUT·OF·THE·JAR·

Out of the Jar. Illustration by Henry Justice Ford (1860-1941) From The Crimson Fairy Book.

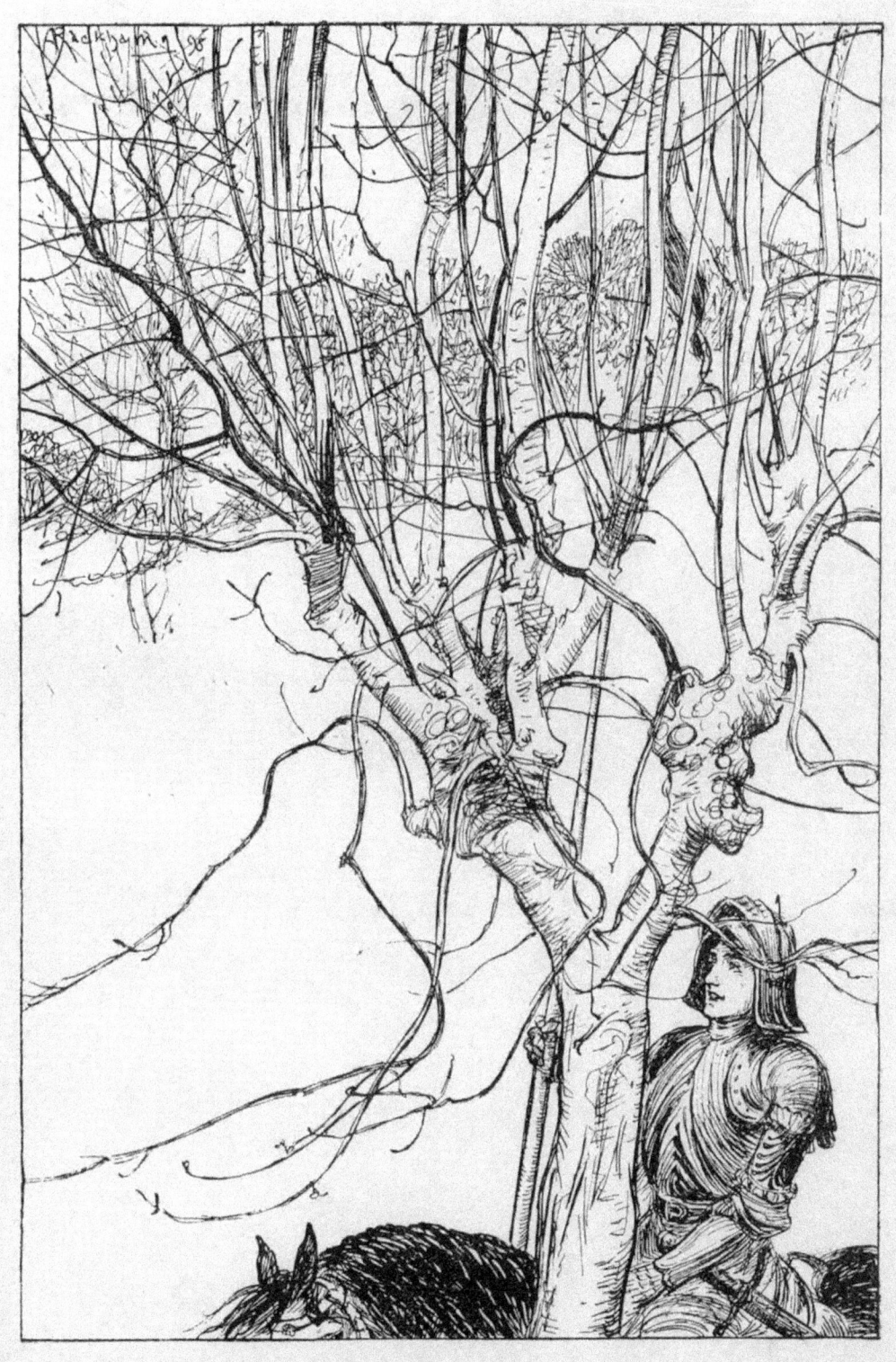

Rode Upon his Way. Illustration by Arthur Rackham (1867-1939) from The Ingoldsby Legends.

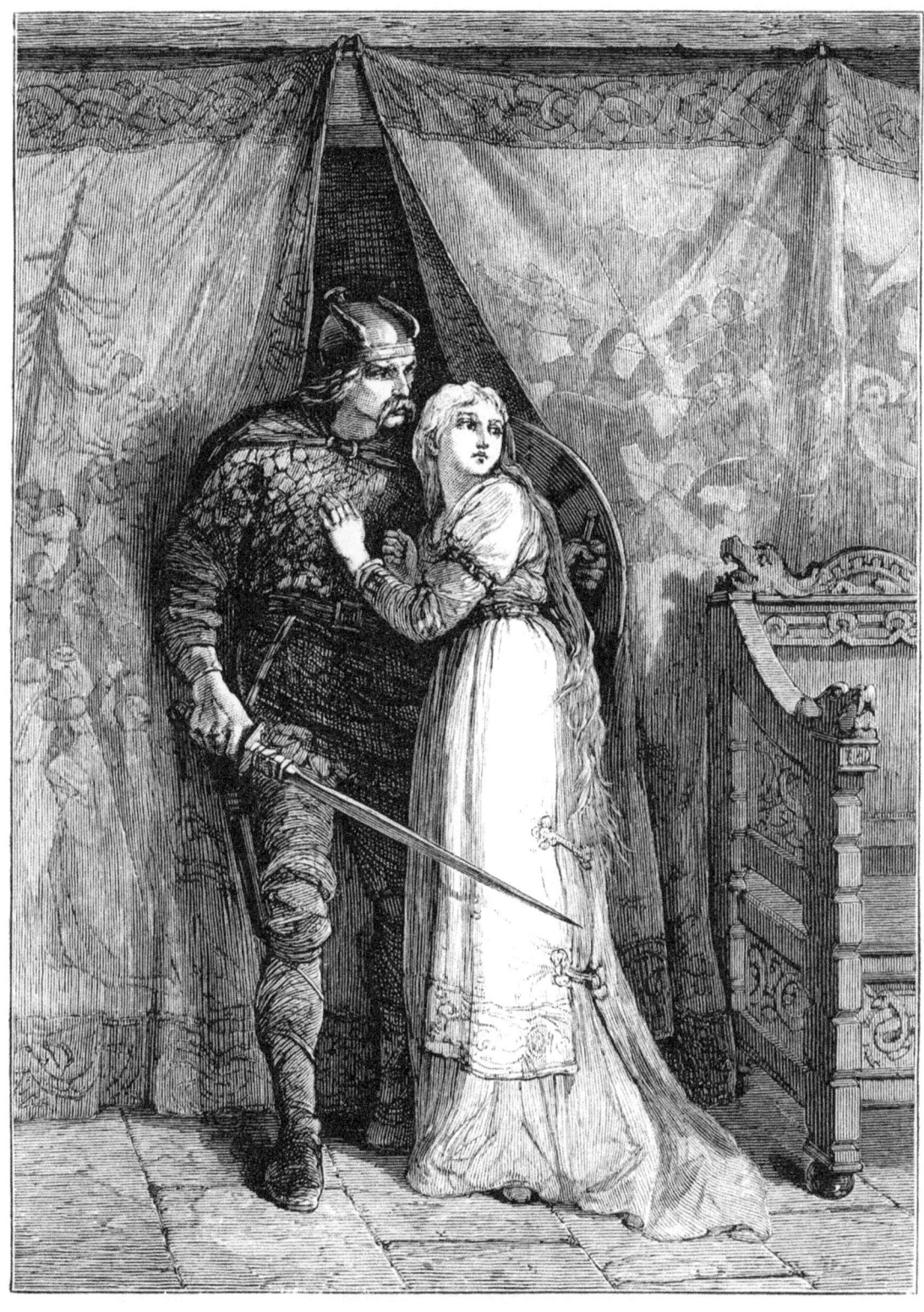

Dove So White. Illustration by Mary A. Hallock Foote (1847-1938) from The Skeleton in Armor.

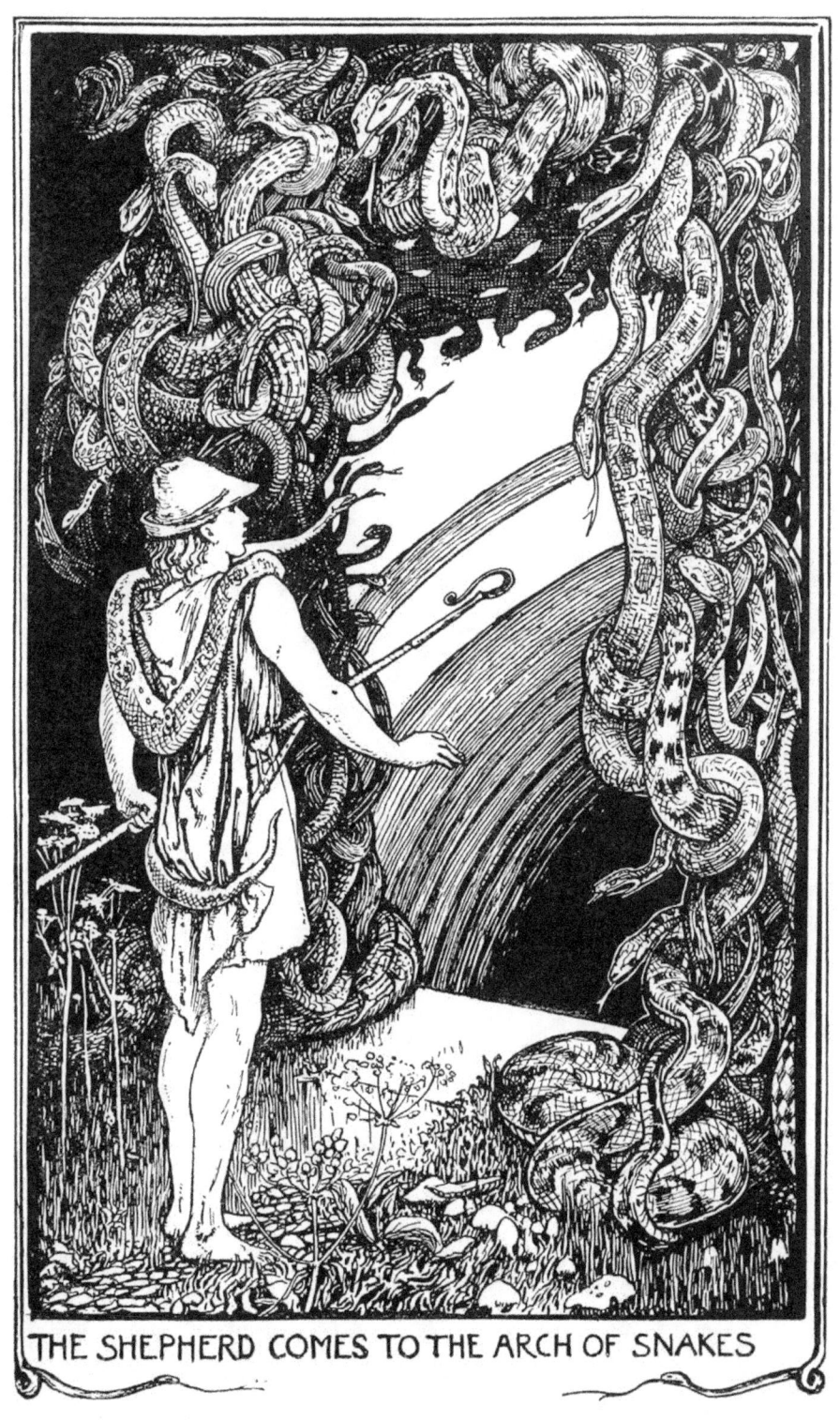

THE SHEPHERD COMES TO THE ARCH OF SNAKES

Illustration by Henry Justice Ford from The Crimson Fairy Book

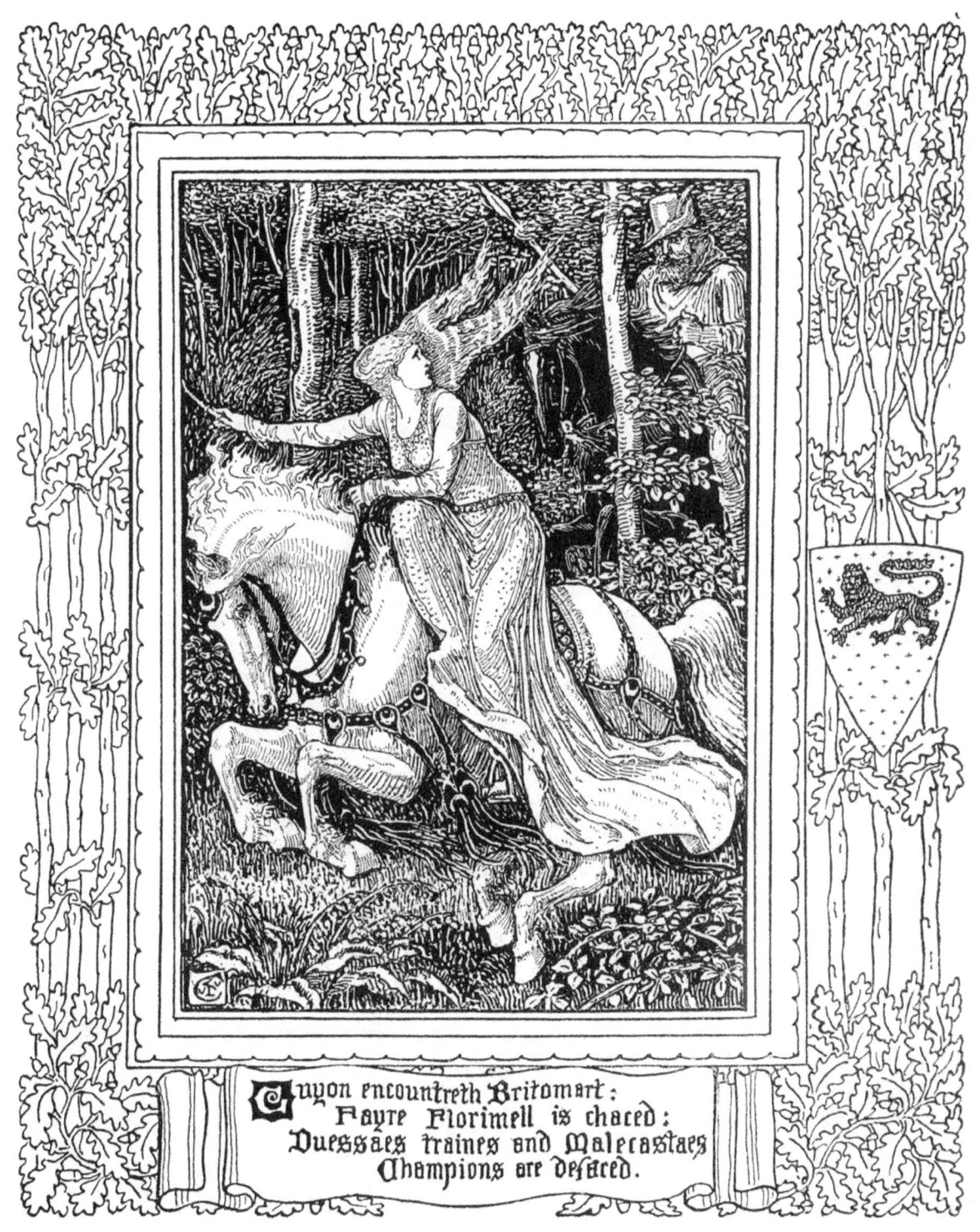

Guyon encountreth Britomart:
Fayre Florimell is chaced:
Duessaes traines and Malecastaes
Champions are defaced.

Fayre Florimell is Chaced. Illustration by Walter Crane (1845-1915), from Spenser's Faerie Queene, vol 3.

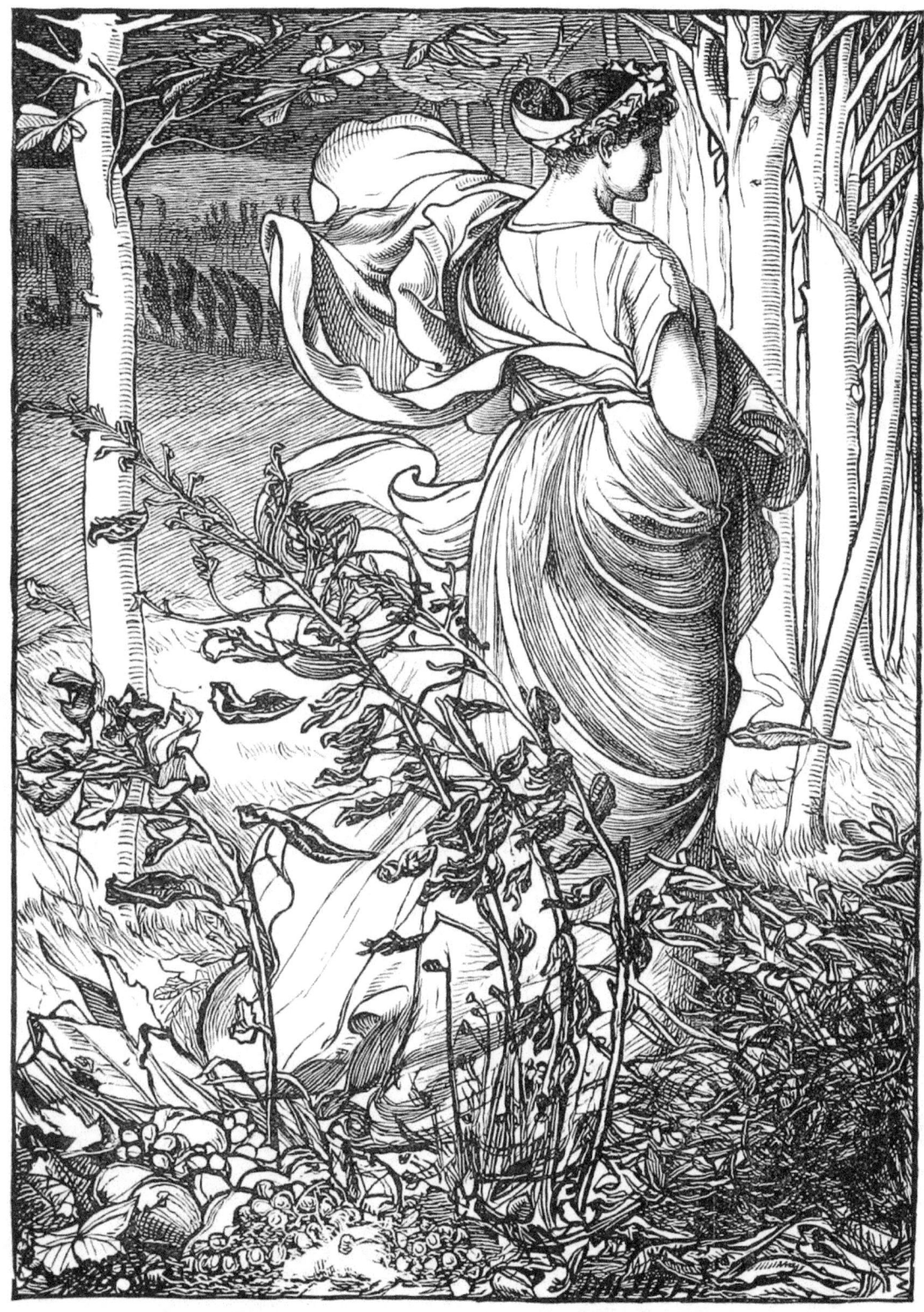

The Advent of Winter. Illustration by Frederick Sandys (1829-1904).

www.ingramcontent.com/pod-product-compliance
Lightning Source LLC
Chambersburg PA
CBHW080608180526
45168CB00007B/2833